PART DARKNESS

PART BREATH

poems

Edward A. Dougherty

Plain View Press
P. O. 42255
Austin, TX 78704

plainviewpress.net
sb@plainviewpress.net
1-512-441-2452

Copyright Edward A. Dougherty, 2008. All rights reserved.
ISBN: 978-1-891386-28-2
Library of Congress Number: 2008927543

Cover art: © Mary Donald, 1994, *Living Inside the Ocean*

Acknowledgements

I am grateful to the editors of the following periodicals for publishing my work and for the long hours, almost always unpaid, bringing poetry to readers.

"Into Darkness," *Poetry East*; "Why I Think About Hiroshima & Nagasaki," *West Branch*; "A Toast," *Rhino*; "The Missing," *Mississippi Valley Review*; "Beth Sleeping, "*Fresh Ground*; "First Frost," *Fathoms*; "Walking Meditation," *Spiral*; "Passing Bell" & "Times Like These," *Three-Lobed Burning Eye*; "Like Superman," *The Other Side*; "Fireflies in the Bamboo Grove," *Parting Gifts*; "Guest" and "How Ants Felled Two Trees," *Barnabe Mountain Review*; "The Stone Circle," *Avocet*; "Grace Street," *Festival*.

The anthology *Atomic Ghost: Poets Respond to the Nuclear Age* included the poem "Why I Think About Hiroshima & Nagasaki."

Thanks to Michael Czarnecki, small-press publisher (FootHills Publishing), poet and Chinese sage living in the hills of upstate New York, for publishing the chapbook *The Metal of My Mouth* in which the following poems appeared: "The Missing," "A Toast," "Speaking for Myself," "Times Like These," "Passing Bell," and "Why I Think About Hiroshima & Nagasaki."

Thanks also go to Christopher Renz, O.P., editor of *Ruah: Journal of Spiritual Poetry* who gave *Small Galaxies* the New Eden Chapbook Award. His sensitive editorial reading is deeply appreciated. The following poems appeared in that collection: "Fishing Boats on the Beach," "How Ants Felled Two Trees," "Fireflies in the Bamboo Grove," "Into Darkness," and section 2 of "Conjunction" was published under the title "Observing Silence."

This book is for Beth

Contents

Part Darkness, Part Breath

    Fishing Boats On the Beach   9
    The Gratitude Papers (I)   10
    Into Darkness   11
    Why I Think About Hiroshima & Nagasaki   13
    Of Wings, Of Opening   15

Fountains & Wildflowers

    The Illustrated Manuscript   19
    Meditation On Marriage   20
    Beth Sleeping   21
    Defining Motion   22
    The Maple Leaf Elegy   23
    First Frost   24
    Bedrock   25
    Walking Meditation   26

The Metal Of My Mouth

    A Toast   33
    Speaking For Myself   37
    The Missing   40
    Times Like These   41
    Passing-bell   42
    Like Superman   43

Signature in Stone

    Story   47
    The Stone Circle   49
    A Way Of Prayer   50

Simplicity	51
The Sound Of Feathers	52
Almost	53
Fossil	55
Fireflies In the Bamboo Grove	56
Celebrating a Reunion	57

Returning to the Seed

Conjunction	61
Passing Steve's Field	65
The Owl Suite	67
By More Than Candlelight Do We Make Love	69
Moments Away	70
Holder Of My Dreams	71
How Ants Felled Two Trees	72
No Room	73
Nothing To Do With Decoration	74
Grace Street	75
Notes	77
About the Writer	79

PART DARKNESS, PART BREATH

Fishing Boats On the Beach

after van Gogh

Crimson like roses. Like our lives,
they are outlined in black, deep and impenetrable.
Blue oars to dip into water
when winds fail. Like the sun
crowning the horizon, these boats
carry such promise. They seem to smile,
filled with something that settles them
into the sand. I think of Jesus

in the tossing prow
while wild animals took up the shape
of the sea. He said his friends
were of little faith, believing so much
in the logic of nature,
of what is most visible.

He rose, spoke to the water and wind,
and they lay down to sleep,
contented. Night gathered around the boat,
leaving the men to wonder
which promise to believe.

The Gratitude Papers (I)

Dawn   what it
suggests   what it regrets

After cold sleep
under flannel   a luxury
I always longed for
and feared

> *"the practice of any virtue*
> *requires a certain*
> *asceticism*
> *and a very definite*
> *leaving-behind*
> *of the niggardly*
> *part of the ego"*

May the miser me
find his cave
his discipline   I bless him
on our way

The candle gives a shadow
more pale   I give a nod
to the sheet-white sky

grateful
for what it brings
what it denies

Into Darkness

—1— Descent
Sometimes when I am breathing carefully, not taking for granted the complexities of that filling and emptying, how molecule by invisible molecule I touch the cottonwood tree quivering in the breeze, sometimes I feel a descent. I sink into an image of darkness. I descend into soil. *God saw that the light was good and God separated the light from the darkness* because *darkness was already with God.* Like breath, it didn't need to be created—both were in God before the beginning. My breathing is sometimes like this, a trail I follow, a river path after flash flooding: willow and brush all tangled and crossed, all pointing in the direction of water's flow. I follow this breathing, this thin strand that comes out of my body and connects me to the world. I think of Beth's cornflower seeds, which breathe even in the dark of their packets at the store. Though they need light, the seeds would burn up if we threw them into the sun, but hidden in the soil, separated from the light, they sprout. They emerge like hands, heels together, palms up ready to catch moisture, sunshine, and the whole breathing world, and funnel it down into the roots, just beginning to reach out. Sometimes when I am breathing carefully, this is what I am.

—2— Only This
In the beginning there was no time
and nothing to measure it with
there was only this

Darkness   closed in around itself
wonderful and perfect

In the darkness there was breathing
it moved through the dark
part darkness and part breath

In the breathing there were waters
over which the breath moved

In the waters there was no violence
as creation had not begun
there was motion but no matter

In the beginning there was radiation
moving in all directions at once

—3— On the Trinity
"*The effects could be called
unprecedented,
magnificent, beautiful, stupendous,*

and terrifying. The whole country

*was lighted by a searing light
with the intensity many times
that of the midday sun. It was golden,*

purple, violet, gray, and blue.

*First the air blast pressed hard against people,
to be followed almost immediately
by the strong, sustained awesome*

roar which warned of doomsday

*and made us feel we puny things
were blasphemous
to dare tamper with the forces*

heretofore reserved for the Almighty."

(General Farrell, Deputy to Manhattan
Project Commander General Leslie
Groves: On the Trinity Test, July 16, 1945)

Why I Think About Hiroshima & Nagasaki

        I'm happy. I've got
        plenty to eat.

Pumpkins cooked
in their shells; potatoes baked
under the hot dirt.

        I wasn't alive, so I
        don't remember.
        1945. War.

"He took a woman by the hands
but her skin…

        Look at these hands,
        they have plenty of fingers.

her skin slipped off
in huge, glovelike pieces."

        My life is good.
        Tony Medwid showed me
        a roofing tile from an old
        Catholic cathedral—the largest
        in Asia. It was ruined
        by the atomic bomb.

Another woman huddled herself
around her child—dead
for four days.

        The clay tile
        had bubbled in the heat.
        Boiled.

She held that baby
even after the body
had begun to decay.

        "Imagine," he said,
        "what would happen
        to the human body."

Of Wings, Of Opening

I dream still of flying   of wings

and something like faith
opening   the strength
the muscular tension of it

     how in the center
there is the elegant
   essential hollow

a blue circle   empty and whole

FOUNTAINS & WILDFLOWERS

The Illustrated Manuscript

             In the round universe
of a capital B, in the letter's tiny top panel,
the astonished soldiers fall away
as streams of light
bore through the rock wall, laying an altogether new
and powerful hand on them, pushing them
into the earth.
             It always begins with touch.
Mary Magdalene, my sister in ivory, falls back
from Jesus' command
             in the lower panel. In artists
words animated this scene again and again
across centuries, and so they painted
"Do not touch me," in gold coins.
Over and over, the flash in the mind:
the gardener is no longer only a gardener.
The touch of an altogether
new awareness. It always begins
in the mind.
             In the heart,
words weigh like a sack of rubies,
a handful of earth, a jar of alabaster.
They no longer reside in any book
but step out of their mourning cloths
and live.
             These days, however,
words are only a shape of light
running across screens, stripped
of their ceramic character,
their fingerprint,
             but in the golden universe
within the black outline
of each life, even now, the brush
is extended to illuminate its story.

Meditation On Marriage

When we were seniors in college,
Paul called to announce
he was getting married. I shame
still to think how I tried to sound
happy, how from the awkwardness
of my own life *marriage*
sounded like a remote
and terrible place.

This summer, with a rare leisure,
I returned to a book about contemplation
read in clearer student days.
Not like readings for class (which I received
with varying success), this book
absorbed me. I could remember

little content, but more
of the context: sunny lawn spots
and peanut butter-and-jelly sandwiches
as I read about meditation.

Paul and Mary celebrated
anniversary after anniversary.
And I now know
marriage isn't something
you *get*. It's more
a habit of attention
returned to, each time rewarded
differently, like prayer. Yes,
a form of prayer.

Beth Sleeping

A door hangs neatly,
balanced
on hinges, easing shut.
Open. The walls
are solid, floors,
foundations. All strong.
Space is left
for doorways
and windows. The wood
breathes wide. Into
what, I don't want
to speculate, but some nights
all the rooms
are filled with pain. Some
with guests. Some
with open meadows.
Pain and wildflowers.

Defining Motion

Snow dust on the spruce trees
catches the light and tosses it back;
oak leaves poke through the thin layer,
brown points in a white cloth.
The yard was not ready for this,
and when I say the yard
I mean me. Last night I spoke my heart
and today I pace the faux-pebbled floor
in the yellow house's glassed-in porch.
My same hollowness, my same whining.
In the fifth grade, we left that address.
You said you want to die first
because I'd be able to cope;
you'd interrogate fate, that recalcitrant mute
as silent as the crows I see
dropping snow as they flap away,
spruce branches springing back.
Inside the confines of the garden's fence,
the kale's still green, *a flash of the eternal*
through the latticework of time
where countermotion creates
harmony, and home
means more than an address.
And when I say home, I mean you.
Maybe I could accept your death,
yes, it's true—all I'd have
is the anguish of grief,
reminders in every coffee mug,
spice jar, trailhead, and state line
where your hand won't be
to hold as I make a wish.
Winter may feel like the absence
of all things July or October,
barrenness its defining feature, longing
its defining motion. But cold's
a companion I can walk with.

The Maple Leaf Elegy

You walk out into startling sunlight,
into shadowed breezes and the sound of water
riding into air and falling again to water,
you stand stunned, in the fire
        and division of a broken age,

in an age of war and preparing for war,
an age like any other, when children
learn to count and sing the alphabet
and expect all that life offers
        in its ripening and falling to earth,

the embrace of earth, the tether of it
on our daily dreams. You catch yourself
in the motion of a falling maple leaf,
its red sharpness, its butterfly flight,
        its rest and final comfort.

For once comforted by these limits, freed
and energized, you now expect your own
temporary and sweet ordinariness.
You expect the sound of water in autumn
        to bring you to tears.

First Frost

The sun covers the red wall
descends slowly, row of bricks
by row, each brightening, almost
glowing. I am going to be late.
A weight within slows me.
Outside, few leaves are left green;
colors flash in the light,
in the wind that slaps me awake.
I hurry up the wood-chip path
where last week's storm—
with the suddenness
and brief power of a summer rain—
streamed some of the mulch away
revealing mud underneath. There, today,
on the dark earth worn smooth:
an intricate design of ice,
a white map, spread flat on the ground.
There are no placenames, no knobs of towns,
only lines, connecting one way
with another, visible in long light
of an autumn morning. As more
make their way into the swirling
world, even this thin map
will melt away, leaving only
the earth we walk on, the wind
we move through, and the light.

Bedrock

I lie on my back on rock that saw
the scrape of glaciers, the long history
of water carrying away layer after soft layer
until this barren bed faced the air.
No water runs now on this side of the stream,
only sky and wind in their dry currents.

I wear boots I thought durable,
a purchase I agonized over.
They carried me though deserts
and across alkaline plains, down a path
edged by ferns and redwoods
to the rocky beach
and the vast, mothering sea.

Now hundreds of miles
from the ocean, in a canyon
cut by water which still runs
in its course, here I lie:
small as the droplets that float out
invisibly from the great falls,
an itch, a breath,
a wink in the eye of stone.

Walking Meditation

> *Although we walk all the time, our walking is*
> *usually more like running.*
> *When we walk like that, we print anxiety*
> *and sorrow on the earth.*
> —Thich Nhat Hanh

—i—

A wind this sharp
this studded should be
illegal   In some places
it is   They drive up
in black cars yank you in
and take you away

Or they roll
dark windows down and gun
across the whole crowd

You know this   You know
the electrodes to the earlobes
the genitals   *Peace* you say
is every step   You know

the danger
is not only outside
in the street
The threat must
begin somewhere

Peace is every step

—ii—
As if the tender one   her lover
were the blade   he ran
the knife along her skin
scratching the bumps of spine
the blue map of veins
along her wrist   her throat

He pressed it against her
until the metal
was no longer cold

He'd gotten in easily   as easily
as the man who broke the window
of an 84-year-old West Toledo woman
That one stole a ten and five ones
from the old woman's purse
after raping her

—iii—
Vietnam is only as far away
as your name
I like your name how
breath begins it
and silence

completes it   Both
have the same shape

I like how delight
and discovery
run naked in the streets

—iv—
Before turning
the video camera on
she testified

her husband
dragged her by the throat
into the bedroom   taped
her mouth and eyes shut

No her husband answered
I didn't rape my wife   How
can you rape
your own wife

—v—
This bitter wind should be outlawed
Now that the pumpkin
wears a white cap of snow   I walk

Cut across backyards   between neighbors'
up the brick street
            —I'm almost running
usually have to wait for the light at Main   then either
across the still-carless parking lot   or straight up
to Saint Aloysius Church and grade school
and angle across the playground   There

I step across the world

—vi—
Where do we start
Like you we are monks
shut up   in our little worlds
of striving

Awareness
What do you mean
Awareness

Could you explain please

Awareness   awareness   awareness

　—*vii*—
In any of the houses on Clough
Prospect   Summit   Railroad
she could slide back
the glass door   step quietly
down a few concrete stairs

Each meeting of foot
with ground   a terror

　—*viii*—
With the war walking freely
harrowing the fields the villages the people
children grew up   used to it
We learn to think violence
is the only way

The holy ones of your monastery decided to leave
decided to walk out of those Buddhist walls

You learned a new way
of awareness   another way
of compassion   No
it didn't stop the killing

You stepped into the war
and took the broken bodies
in your arms

because peace
because healing
because

it is the only way
to begin

THE METAL OF MY MOUTH

A Toast

> *The cup is filled with night*
> —Bei Dao

—i—
Keep your head down   Look
for your feet   Behind the trees
smoke thickens   rises   a curtain

Tracers in the sky
make beautiful fireworks
Opening night   A kind of wedding

celebrating our lives together   All the songs
echo with explosions   Keep your head
down and don't look too far ahead

—ii—
Fingers, lips: I chew myself open until the dusty metal
of blood fills my mouth. Each day I think *we are going
to war*. At night I toss awake: darkness and the oil
of dreams wash me; the hollowness of something missing,
a tooth, a leg below the knee joint, an eye.

The socket throbs. Conversations circle
a black pond: waters we wade through
into a place where people wake up
to the best way to survive, the best way
to turn flesh to emptiness, the quickest way.

The taste will not wash out of our mouths:
the violence we accept
we will again inflict, again.

The cup of darkness, the bitter
hollowness,
is raised.

—*iii*—

In a letter to his mother Wilfred Own wrote,
   Here is a gas poem,
        done yesterday.

—*iv*—

Here is how we pray in the holy place:
   choking on our own lungs.

Here is how we speak to the blue savior:
   high choir of missiles and jets.

The flames of mercy are damp:
   we kill the young to save their purity.

—*v*—

the chant of ages I dream
the blue rain of trees I dream
I dream the sweetness of my own limbs

tomorrow is a wagon of pain
tomorrow is a burn mark on the earlobe
tomorrow is a broken bottle thrust into the body

I dream the chant of parents
fathers sleepless in sweaty beds I dream
mothers pacing the night orange
I dream the sweet grey strokes of noon

because the terror is in our mouths
the sorrow   because the nightmares
the nightmares live in our mouths

from the sweetness of my own dreams
I chant the dreams of children

—vi—
Low to the water   wooden piers
echo my steps   Fine woven reeds
white baskets float   water to the lip

The faces of infants   still visible
under the glass-pane of water
Our skin   One basket
just below the surface
You're stripping away
our human skin
sinks below sight

Warrior boats glide in
over night-still waters
spear points glinting

I wish our love
for peace was an offering
not a jewel to be protected

—vii—
Each morning I wake thinking
we're at war, and all day
I am swimming, shoulders raw with the work,
feet dipping—every motion a decision.
I am a poor swimmer, and this pond of fear
is deep as grief, only more tentative.
I receive a book ordered weeks ago;
I hold it, crack open the stiff pages
marveling how a person worked
and reworked these words, and someone else

bound them together
so I could sit at the edge of my bed
holding the pulpy cover, tracing the pressed letters.

For the rest of the day, at work or walking,
I think of the blue cover with thick ivory pages
anticipating how experience
walks in such words. It is a joy
despite how tentative feelings are, despite how momentary
everything has become, despite what will begin to appear—
things that will take shape in letters and words,
things we'll have to swim to,
working, to feel.

—*viii*—

Here is how we kneel at the stone altars:
   fingernails ploughing our necks, our tight, tight throats.

Here is how we proclaim the Gospel:
   frothy lips kiss the clouds.

The flames of understanding are damp:
   kill the young, save their purity.

Speaking For Myself

> *The supreme political fact of our lives is the atomic bomb. Am I wrong? It is enormous; it occupies the world. It is not only what it is but also the concentrated symbol of all hatred and injustice in every social and economic sphere. Speaking for myself, I have lived in fear of it for fifteen years, fear that it will go off, one way or another, and kill me and my family, or render our lives so intolerable that we won't wish to go on. Maybe I am more timorous than most people; I believe there are actually more Americans who never think about the bomb. But poets?*
>
> —Hayden Carruth (1961)

I am writing the bomb. I am always
getting bigger because I am writing
the bomb in my belly, the targeted,
the locked behind a series
of coordinated commands bomb.
Am I more fearful than most, more
fearsome or troublesome? Am I
rolling in my hands a fact,
making a mountain
out of a footnote? I am writing
the history of a metal, a filling
in my mouth throbbing
with threat. I want to grab you
by the scruff of your threatened neck.
I want to take you by the hand.
I want more than is possible?
What is possible inside this
ruling? A crooked measure
of what's good to eat, what to wear
against the wind, the snow
that is so much like a drift
of ashes. The white shadow
on my X-ray, Kodak knew

was coming. In a locked drawer
in Pennsylvania's low mountains,
the black plains, the dark sheets
of film spotted, as if spores
of fungus blew in
through the many black holes
in the telephone. Another voice
calling for an appointment
with Doctor Bomb. Prescribe
the bomb, write it down before
it goes off. Again. Write it. Here,
take my testimony: we knew.
All along, we knew. All along
the glittering rivers of Hiroshima
when the Army doctors
paraded those little girls to take
their clothes off for the camera,
when the desert air crackled
with scriptures, when the silos
hollowed out an enormous tube
in the great prairies of the earth,
when a report sighed as it slipped
out of the manila envelope
only to be sent away Dismissed! with words
it could not grasp. Next! I read about
one man's fear and that primitive
longing to write himself into—...
and out of the bomb comes
a burning wind, a dark wall
that rolls over the civilized miles,
writing rubble in the cities
and writing on the living things
What have we done? Oh my God
I am heartily sorry for having
this bomb inside me
and for the thoughts

for which it stands, one policy
underground, one last stand
selling hot dogs outside the stadium
and the crowds inside
already cheering, thumping
on the bleachers, a blinding white
page and the sky is as blue
as ever and the autumn day
as crisp as a crimson maple leaf
and under my head my fingers
go to sleep inside the droning
of a single plane overhead
from the county airport
its white trail writing
my history. Again. Write it.

The Missing

Everything everything comes back   returns
to the deaths the deaths   missing
Everything will be all right   Will everything
Don't worry   Try to get some sleep
How can we sleep   When everything
comes back will it have its place
It turns on a gap   empty gap
the desk empty   space on the elevator everything
comes back to the deaths the silences
holes in sentences in language   the deaths
holes in newspapers where photos go
where photos   where go   gaps
talk in the family   the bedroom
empty   the bed straight and neat
Will everything be all right   Will everything
sleep when it returns from death   Is there a quilt
in the empty bedroom   trophies   shoes
in the closet   Is there a silence
where words used to move   water
dripping water in the sink
the faucet dripping words   tapping stainless steel
words   bedrooms   closets   shirts   elevators
desks   shoes   newspapers   silence
everything comes back   Will everything
be all right   Don't worry

Times Like These

> *I think it better that in times like these*
> *A poet's mouth be silent, for in truth*
> *We have no gift to set a statesman right...*
> —Yeats, "On being asked for a War Poem"

His voice is electric, crackling
in waves from Washington to London,
from Baghdad to Beijing.
Metal and buzzing.
                    The statesman
opens his mouth and people
turn to shadows
            on bank steps—
  as Blake said,
  'And the hapless soldier's sigh
  Runs in blood down palace walls.'

Sand, dust, and skin flaking off in rafts
fill the air, cloud airways, stick
in thick mouths until voices rasp,
whisper, and go mute.
                    And so,
before my silence is enforced,
I raise my voice, offer what gift,
no matter what it does
to the statesman.
        I
  must be made
            more human.
  Silence
        is for stones.

Passing-bell

> *What passing-bell for these who die as cattle?*
> *Only the monstrous anger of the guns.*
>   —Wilfred Owen "Anthem for Doomed Youth"

Under the weight of misty streets and lights
I say   I do not believe
I will not obey   Others will but
I will not follow into the dark neighborhood
My name has been forgotten   all our names

I cannot contain my rage   It spills out
It runs down streets   streets dark as polished marble
Streets closed in like hospital halls
My rage etches names in the night   My rage
catches like orders in my throat like curses
But stops   choking   I know I am not innocent

But I will not stop my anger

I am a bell   the metal of my mouth rings
it rings like sign faces hit with a fist
it rings like hubcaps pelted with stones
there are so many ways to die   I am a bell

the heavy clapper swings

a bell's weight   cannot be measured   its weight
is darkness   darkness   dense as absence
dark as closed malls   dark like the shadows
under bridges   dark as mouths
mouths open to the night   open in rage
rage etching names into the night   rage
etching all our names into solid night

Like Superman

I know I'm just flapping my arms here,
he said, but I don't want no parts
of any turkey shoot. He said

he used to dream of flying, not in planes,
but walking down the neighborhood,
taking a few steps and actually

lifting off. Like Superman, he said,
like Superman. I never wanted to be
in the Air Force, his voice getting small

in a cell somewhere in Germany.
Now Rob wants another war
so he can go, and a woman in the room says,

when you get on TV, don't be boring.
We don't want our wars
boring, our press conferences dull,

our generals too mundane. We want
soldiers who can describe the action
like sports announcers. "It's like," they say,

"It's like a turkey shoot." All those birds
flapping their useless wings. These people
can't fly F-15s, and they can't

run away fast enough. So he sits in his cell
somewhere far from the journalists' pool,
bored, waiting for the military court

to accuse him of not killing anyone.

SIGNATURE IN STONE

Story

The room was not crowded; people scattered
in the folding chairs in twos and threes.
Anne Coleman shied from the microphone,
but took it and told about her daughter,
Frances, dead eleven years, told
about the overworked and therefore
callous police—a process, she said,
that created not justice but rage,
a blue and burning rage. They could give
only four days to each case
with all the other murders going on.

The killer was never caught.
Some shook their heads at this.
The stillness was complete listening.

The wellspring of anger continued
to bubble up in their lives
until it consumed her son.
Two years after his sister's funeral,
Daniel killed himself. Some of us
wept, but Anne Coleman was done
with tears. She continued to tell.
And all the while this story
of sorrow was carving a space
in us. Even as we gained details
and understanding, something
slipped out of us with the current.

Years later, she met another mother
whose son was about to die. "The State,"
Anne told us, "was deliberately
going to kill in my name."
She knew the absence in the heart,

the gap in the family,
about to be created, she knew
the rage, so she visited every inmate
on death row, she wore placards
to stop the killing. She—
who'd lost so much—asked us
to acknowledge our place
"in the chain of violence."

And now when I hear
words like *murder* or *vengeance*,
but especially *forgiveness*
that space hollowed out
by this story
suddenly
     and completely
               fills up

and the story begins to move

like an animal
     roused from sleep.

The Stone Circle

Because of the invisible words beneath these

the muffled voices behind our small
black walls   walls once open
to sudden solstice light

Because blue waves of liquid glass

turn over our lives and break
slowly into air while we fall back
into habits and phrases as if inevitably

Because the prairie wind becomes voices

murmuring over stone circles
tracing the sun's motion
over hundreds of human generations

Because of these enormous personal silences

we need a moment   a true and calm
         gold-yellow gleam
a way in a way out

A Way Of Prayer

The old woman
at Butsuji
stood before
an iron pot
of ashes. Great
plumes of incense.

She cupped hands
and brought
the smoke up
and around
her head,
to her body, blessing
herself
with fragrance.

Simplicity

A Franciscan wood-dark cell
in the thick of the birdsong forest.
"Have you ever tasted
water earth-cool, fresh
from the well?"

She lived there with a copy
of Clare's writings
and a magnolia tree
which only barely bloomed.

The silent chapel
has remained with
and within me
all these years.

The Sound Of Feathers

A chickadee comes to the just-leafing
crab-apple and blesses me
with its two-syllable song
   —as if the language of birds
were measured by ours. The air recalls
the way it feels warm when snow
in stillness begins to fall.
I've been reading books by men who knew
they faced passing out of this

amazement, this tapestry. The sparrows
arrive all crackling, bobbing on thin branches.
Their feathers ruffle
and I think of dying. Losing all this.
   —And the words hunch away
into the grind and rumble

of the garbage truck, the road crew
chewing up then laying down Water Street,
and the chickadee who returns
with its two-note song.

Almost

> *If someone had told us then*
> *you would die in nineteen years,*
> *would it have sounded*
> *like almost enough time?*
> —Donald Hall "Letter in the New Year"

Seeing a tuft of fur on the highway shoulder
—brick-red, brown, blackened by oil
and sun—struck me wordless, numb.
An appropriate hollowness
had filled the morning, growing as heat
spread into shade. Somehow,
without knowing when
or how, we had opened the door
to death and now it inhabits us.
Your colleague's husband. Genevieve
killed at noon by a drunk driver.
The birds we draw to feeders, one's head
picked to a small, white ball.
Even the kitten we adopted
from the dairy farmer. Grief eroded me
in ways I never knew, so I tried to reason:
She was just an animal
      —as if you are anything else.
We knew it was coming
      —who wrote 'our steps are brief'?
All we could do was fill ourselves
with cheap wine and the night
with talk of other encounters.
Death is a feast we can only take in portions.
Kitten, father, sister, grandfather, cousin.
You cried yourself to sleep
imagining being left without me.
All morning, I drove with the taste of loss
in my mouth until passing

a row of three Mountain Ash trees
with their orange fruit glowing in the light
—somehow the beauty of it
broke me. Tears salt-burned my eyes.
At lunch we held each other,
swaying in a hug that will not
last forever, not even in memory.

Fossil

The shell will leave a sign   Each layer
each day-worn worry   however slight is a weight
I wrestle under   struggling and rolling
in a slice of light the color of seawater

I resist the comfort of sleep   that quality of night
that redeems darkness   I am tearing
out my heart again   It takes a long time
for sleep to settle   like the sea shifting
in its tides   slowly laying sediment over the living

Abandoned by life   the shell
will leave its signature in stone   and I
in a seatide motion am alive

There is something constant in the drifting dark
Breathing with the slow rhythm of sleep
you have floated off   leaving your book
like a bird   hovering over you

The world was born   of water of the sea
and of necessity   learned to fly
to ride the motion of air   to breathe it directly

Fireflies In the Bamboo Grove

The cicadas were still
grinding away the afternoon.
A single one would do.

Slender poles in the wind.
The pond a shadow.
Invisibly, water eased itself
into that dark bowl.
Lilies were dull sticks, knobbed
where blossoms once were.

Every day this summer
green ran off, abandoning us like this.
Then, yellow lights in that hollow—
so much, so lively. And out of that motion,

a lightness came

up out of the grasses that had blackened
in the night, out from the arching bamboo itself.

Celebrating a Reunion

It is this way in the old churches
where readers climb to the lectern,
making the faithful tip back
their heads and the words shower down.

There are so many meanings,
so many passionate
ways to understand. Clouds
pile up their substance
and emptiness, their dense,
vaporous bodies, all feathered
and lovely in the blue plains.

Jesus said to be like
the Compassionate One who gives
rain to the just
and unjust equally. I learn again
(each time new), climbing
together with you to places
we may have been before:

love is a single thing;
its many passionate meanings
will not be exhausted.

RETURNING TO THE SEED

Conjunction

for John Bradley

—1— *To John, This Offering*
Returning to friendship, a force that sustained
across hemispheres and the demonic rage of history,
to tears and the wrestle of dreams,
neither of which I understand,

Returning to the most intimate conjunction
Because I was listening to other things, other ways of knowing,

Returning to a place where names
are unreadable, where slate-blue rivers
run calmly through the reflective, shimmering mind,

Returning to the conjunction and green flame
of the self, to grammar
we can never escape, to a dawn
crimson with confusion,

Returning to the rhythm of a phrase
that is both disturbing and beautiful,

Returning to a raging habit that breaks my heart
but I fall back into like sleep,

Returning to offer you this:

Because there are invisible words under these,

Because Kobodaichi sat on the mountain
without food or water for one hundred days,

Because his fire still burns on Miyajima,
tended by monks and devout laypersons
hundreds of years later, and because

There is no other word for because…

—2— *Returning to August 6*
I was listening to other things,
eyes closed for other sight.
The cicadas had stopped.

The superfortress has been up there for hours
heading this way. The war has been over for years.

At the news, each member of the family, starting
with grandfather, rose and reached for the other.
Holding hands, they observed

Silence. Listening for other things.
My eyes were closed but I could see.

Clinging to bark, the cicadas had stopped.
The great thrumming of engines
filled the heavy chamber of a still summer evening.

Why return to this approaching? Why let years
circle like a stunned family? I have no answer but

Silence like a kind of listening. The world
and all its paces tuned to a pitch
just out of reach, a band of color just out of range.

—3— The Hungry Ghosts
The old monk said the streets are thick with them, wandering
  homeless. They grope,
desperate to be at peace, ghosts in a world that does not believe in
  ghosts. You must be careful,
walking, driving, even bundling along the arcade, shopping, you
  must take great care. Every step
is shadowed by their ghostly fingers grasping the air turned by your
  passing pant leg.
Every step you take in this city where you are an alien. Your
  decisions, take care:
how you choose and what. As you move from task to task, filling
  your hours
with meetings and happenings, you are pages ahead of the seasons,
  miles ahead of your souls.
This is the space they inhabit, the kingdom you don't even know
  about let alone rule.
The old monk says the more we dismiss as superstition, the more
hungry and desperate their longing, the more we owe them. In this
  city, the blind monk said,
the streets are thick with these ghosts, yearning to be at peace,
  longing to come home.

—4— The Place of the Seed
I am told that seeds   buried in earthen walls
seeds dormant for years   burst open
   in the sun-centered heat

Listening   that dry yet accessible place
I am leaning close   listening
   to walls and ghosts

Returning   a long slow circle
in the wrestle of history   I am returning
   to my life the larger one

I am returning   to the place of that seed
the shriveled homeland   the spirit-clogged place
   I am coming home here to live

Passing Steve's Field

The fiddle began with the most obvious
before taking on the more difficult truths:
there is nothing to be afraid of.

The low spring sun was warm, laying
soft color along the yellow-budding hills.
On 228 between Alpine and Trumansburg
a field of ruined farm machines

took on a glow of achievement, of a job
done well, not only to work the land
but to mine it and shape its metals.
And now that it's accomplished,
the human labor can't bear the sun
in its May orbit. I've started calling it

Steve's Field because he first drew
my attention to the range of rusted beauty. Death
takes many avenues, and none of them
really quick; in the meantime,

there is music from Cape Breton Island,
the smile on Beth's face, head bobbing
to the music, and the way
love sometimes feels like a hillside
swaying in the sunset. The fiddle
proceeded to the slower, harder truths,
the more elusive ones, like renewal.
Going up to have dinner with Steve,
friendship was breaking open

in another dying American town.
And for weeks, we'd been feeling
our own germination, even as
we moved (again)

all our boxes of books and pottery and
cookware and all the other things
we only partly own
and are owned in part by.

By the time the fiddler moved out of the Air
and into the next section, we too ached with joy
as we hurtled down a New York sideroad:
we felt the thrill of a whole crowded hall
bursting into applause
as she began dancing as she played,
the music of another kind of spring.

The Owl Suite

owl, the hunter
Owl wears its mask of night like me
speaking many voices listening
in the clump of trees hearing

how everything was flattened *everything*
to the earth another circle of houses
another supermarket sickly pines

and a stand of scrub oak low bushes
Virginia creeper uniting one
to the next like a voice

Owl the hunter clings to brittle branches
hides itself against the trunk hides itself
in its own colors its own soft feathers

the moment
Owl arranges winter's
blue fringe, the bleak
and crumbling evening. I, the owl,

am wide-eyed and motionless.

Through dry oak leaves, the wind
hisses its prophesy. Clouds cover
and reveal the studious moon.

In this thicket, I sit and watch.

Water trickling through pipes.
Tick, tick, ticking, the clock
betrays the moment's

intimate, green expanse.

watching and knowing
Morning and evening are nothing
to protect: they are not my territory.

But flannel night (when a single
candle overpowers a roomful

of darkness; when the body
in its open cells embraces another

way of knowing); there,
I have seen you.

I watch over your soft departure,
watch as you face another world:

your breathing becomes that sound
of trust, a forest beside me.

By More Than Candlelight Do We Make Love

Our hands
speak, our faces.
Your long hair
now cut close;

my eyes you call
yours, naked now
without glasses.

Yellow-gold light
on white roses:
witnesses
to our bed-night
conversations.

Moments Away

Windows open. The day
like a smooth glass tube.
In chilled hands, a cup of tea.
Warm. Sweet. Through lingering flavor
of garlic, expansive and airy
in my mouth. Earlier, over lunch,
we looked into each other
—a thrill
of being known, tasted,
and yet still yearned after.
I longed for our low bed,
legs entwined, kisses—long
and familiar and like nothing else.
May. Overcast and breezy.
All morning, all afternoon
rain seemed moments away,
like a wish floating off
on the white arms
of the dandelion seed.
Inside, the cats are all
twitch and waiting;
sparrows on the feeder
sing and sing and sing.

Holder Of My Dreams

She holds the tiny dill seeds,
scatters them along the fence.

I want to make my life
a gesture like that. Together
"we are a multitude,"
just as Ovid said.

When she reads aloud
on car trips across states,
she does all the voices,

and I am happy with her
all along the way.

How Ants Felled Two Trees

Before the circling wind let loose
its hungry pack of dogs

Before the rain weighed everything down with grief

Before the upper-atmosphere currents
aligned themselves
for acrimonious stillness

Before summer became what it is

There were ants

Black and numerous like drops of blood, like omens,
ants following the invisible trails
laid down by the bodies of their fellow ants
to the exposed heart of the sweetgum tree.

Each creature took only what it could bear,
no more and no less.

I don't know how the bark
was opened, but it was enough.

And before the ants,
before that engineered line of thieves,
there was a fragrance, a sweetness
going out into the world.

No Room

Just as the wall confirms
the universe   opening

a space for entering   the window
drinks in the wind tossing

the high sunflower heads
one thing

so like another   no room
for deceit or artifice

Nothing To Do With Decoration

for Mary Donald

The sea crumples
             and rises up
of it
    the pelican and hermit crab

With metal
          you can shape
your life into any form
                  except joy
That must soften
           of its own fire

Art-making
          like lovemaking
has nothing to do with
                 accessories
It is soul-beauty
            and it is commitment
to live by it
         in things and in selves

Crafting their own
               sharp lives
barrel cactuses
          in the dry Texas hill country
    flower by it

Grace Street

> *we are a multitude*
> —Ovid

where we prepare an empty house that stood hollow & quiet for months
    seeming to wait for us
where the sander stripped thresholds
    filling the air with wood-dust fine as pollen
where we unpack the mask of Tengu from his wooden box
    and set him to guard against evil
    hanging from the thermostat
where we live, and so we live, crowded together by passions

where, in the tired ease after work, we hear the doorframes
    how they remember the sound of a fist
    hitting a woman's face
where we join the doors in their resolve
    to receive such suffering
    and respond with hospitality
    and the stories feel it and come to warm themselves

where sparrows bring their hearty expectations
and co-workers find a scroll
    that answers a longing
    they can only weep to comprehend
where a friend's mother can leave like an offering
    one small, sharp detail from divorce
where a kitten lives and dies
    and is buried under green feathers
    and the wind's occasional song
    and the watchful eye of sunflowers
where a toad can tunnel a secret home in cedar mulch

where we shot darts at politicians on TV
        and they stuck, they stuck
where we share the same couch to watch a movie
        leaving the other furniture to fend for itself.

where lies are not welcome
where a listening sometimes emerges
        like Don's Russian tomato plant in the compost
        and we hear a rustling
        and move forward with strange confidence

where the mockingbird casts handfuls of musical pebbles down
              the chimney
and the oriole spends a few weeks
        stringing garlands from the locust tree
        then leaves us silence for the summer where its song once was

Notes

"The Gratitude Papers." The italicized Flannery O'Connor quote is in Lewis Hyde's *The Gift*, a book my cousin Kate urged me to read. Hyde confirmed and articulated inklings I'd been yearning toward. He expresses the posture toward life and writing I continue to seek.

"Fishing Boats on the Beach." I carried with me to Hiroshima a small book of van Gogh's work highlighting his final years; my title copies his painting's name.

"The Defining Motion." The italicized quotation is from Joseph Campbell.

"Walking Meditation." Includes passages from a news report, from Anthony DeMello's *One Minute Wisdom*, and Thich Nhat Hanh's *Peace is Every Step*.

"Why I Think…" Passages and images from John Hersey's *Hiroshima*. I wrote this long before considering moving to Japan. During the Celebration of Hope reading, poet and *hibakusha* Hiromu Morishita read a translation while I read the original, marking the fiftieth anniversary by joining American and Japanese, observer and witness, and one generation with another

"A Way of Prayer." Butsuji is an ancient Zen temple complex; the scene described is a quite common Buddhist practice at temples all over Japan.

"Conjunction." *"Because there is no other word for because"* comes from a John Bradley poem. John came to Hiroshima as part of the World Friendship Center's events to mark the 50th anniversary of the atomic bombing. The 10-day Celebration of Hope included a bi-lingual poetry reading featuring work from John's anthology *Atomic Ghost*. Kobo Daishi, inventor of Japan's lettering system and itinerant monk, has many legends associated with him; he did

77

visit Miyajima, though, and the fire was still smoldering when we climbed Mount Misen some 800 years later.

"Grace Street." Tengu, a Japanese guardian spirit often associated with mountain regions, has a frightening nose and fierce expression. The mask is a gift from Yoko Kawakami, and it should have been hung outside, by the front door, so as to keep our home safe from marauding spirits.

About the Writer

After finishing his MFA in Bowling Green, Ohio, Edward Dougherty and his spouse were volunteers at a peace center in Hiroshima for two and an half years. They now live and work in Corning, New York and are active in their Quaker Meeting. Dougherty is the author of *Pilgrimage to a Gingko Tree* (2008 WordTech Communications) and four chapbooks of poetry, the most recent of which is *The Luminous House* (2007 Finishing Line Press). He is also co-author, with Scott Minar, of the textbook, *Exercises for Poets: Double Bloom*, available from Prentice-Hall. In 2007, he was given the SUNY Chancellor's Award for Excellence in Scholarship and Creative Activities. Essays, book reviews, and samples of other work are available by visiting www.edward-dougherty.net.

www.ingramcontent.com/pod-product-compliance
Lightning Source LLC
Chambersburg PA
CBHW071028080526
44587CB00015B/2539